Dedicated with love to my children
Naama, Alma and Oren

"The flowers appear on the earth,
The time of the singing bird has come,
The voice of the turtle-dove is heard in the land"
(Song of Songs, 2:12)

Talia Berkovich-Zehavi
WHO IS SITTING AT MY WINDOW?

Contact to: bztalia@gmail.com
http://www.bztalia.wix.com/books

ISBN-13: 978-1492743767
ISBN-10: 1492743763

Puplished in Israel 2013

WHO IS SITTING AT MY WINDOW?

Written and photographed by:

Talia Berkovich-Zehavi

Translated from Hebrew: **Sharon Blaukopp**

Coo, coo, coo , Coo, coo, coo

Something suddenly

disturbed my sleep,

So to move the curtain I did creep,

And from the windowsill I peeped.

Lo and behold

a bird building a nest,

Piling twigs,

clearing a place to rest,

For a pair of eggs she soon will lay,

In the middle of a bright blue day.

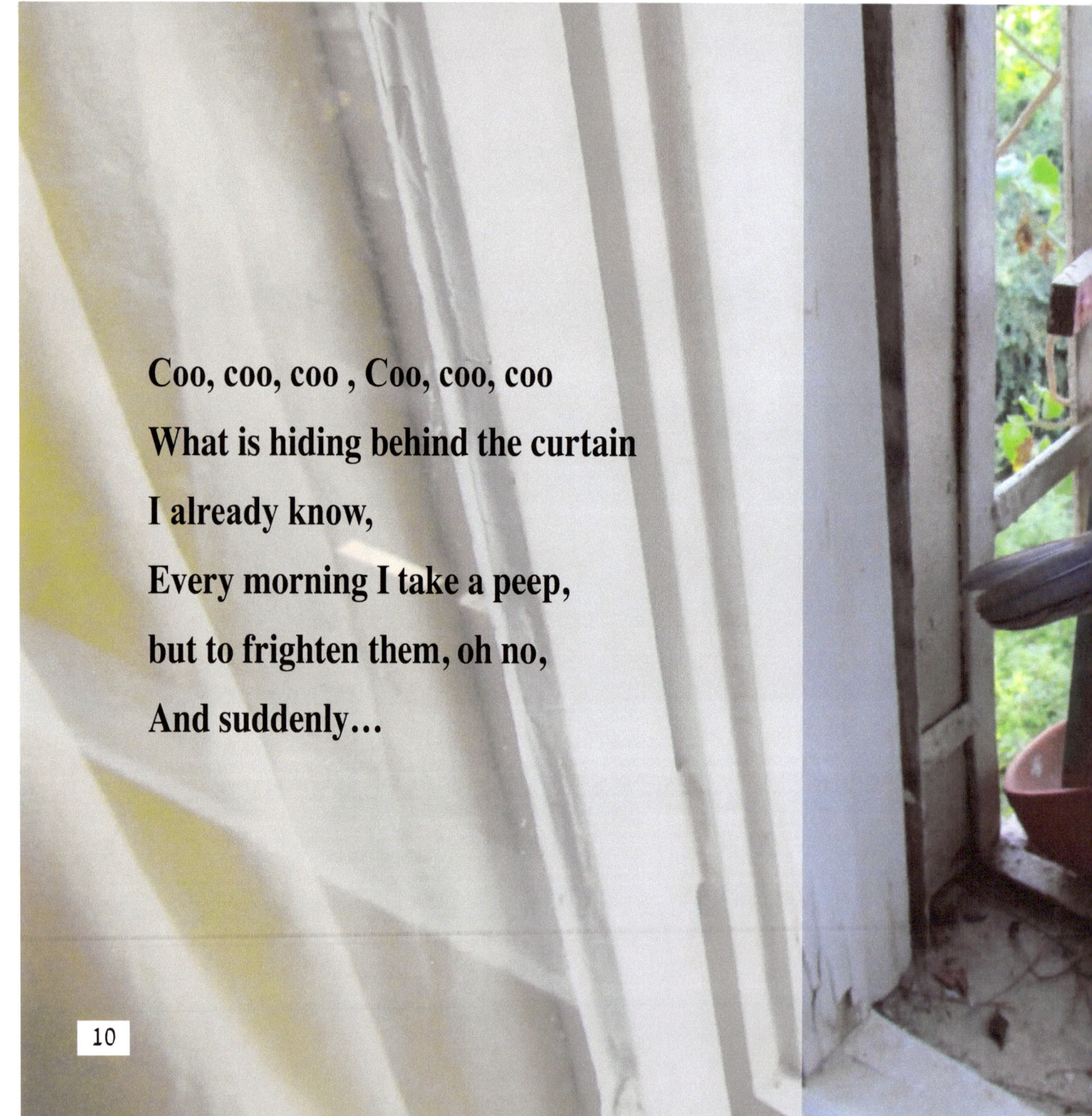

Coo, coo, coo , Coo, coo, coo

What is hiding behind the curtain

I already know,

Every morning I take a peep,

but to frighten them, oh no,

And suddenly…

10

Today,

two white eggs I do see,

Perfectly round, as round as can be.

13

Coo, coo, coo , Coo, coo, coo

A bird sitting on its eggs, oh what a sight,

To watch her just sit and sit day and night,

It looks like a laughing-dove*;

I think I'm right.

*The laughing-dove/wild pigeon/palm-dove is from the pigeon family and is commonly found in Israel.

15

Its color is a beautiful grayish brown,

With a bluish red stripe all the way down,

With black feathers around its neck,

Like an expensive piece of jewelry

she is bedecked,

When her tail she spreads its span,

It opens like a white hand-held fan.

Now her eyes from side to side do dart,

She has something to say rather smart,

Perhaps to Daddy dove she wants to tell,

That he must take a turn as well,

She sat on the eggs all night and

she now of him must ask,

If his turn has arrived to share the task.

Coo, coo, coo , Coo, coo, coo

What do I see emerging

from behind the curtain?

Male or female chick I cannot say for certain,

Which one with joy will burst?

Which one will tire and go to sleep first?

Finally the chicks – out they came,

What they looked like had no name,

They were like two cocoons

 ready to crack,

With soft feathers covering

their entire back.

With their eyes closed at first,

And yellow down from their backs did burst,

After their eyes opened so clear,

Their bodies suddenly were dressed

with feathers so dear.

I know, Zippy and Zip, their names will be,

For all the happiness they have brought to me.

Wrapped together all day in a tight mass,

Hardly moving, and sleeping,

letting the time pass,

Unlike I and my sister who always fight,

They get along fine, oh what a sight,

My mother's advice, oh what a gem,

"It won't harm you to learn

something from them."

They notice whenever I am too near,

As their breast they puff up out of fear,

Also their mother when she saw me at first,

Was stricken by panic, fearing the worst,

Her whole body began to swell and rise,

And with a clap of her wings away

she flew into the skies,

I thought she'd abandoned her chicks,

heaven forbid,

But in fact, to return is what she did.

31

Coo, coo, coo , Coo, coo, coo

Scared of me the two birds definitely are,

Since they swell their bodies to keep me afar,

Their mother taught them many many things,

One was, be careful of strangers who don't have wings.

They must think I am a falcon,

raven or perhaps a crow,

Who is coming to eat them in one blow,

They don't understand that

I mean no harm, only good,

And biscuits I would give them, if only I could.

When my mother heard my idea she laughed and said:

"Their meal is not biscuits nor salads nor bread,

Mother bird takes care of all their needs,

For first course into their throat she drops grains and

some seeds,

For the second course some tiny insects in their tummy,

And perhaps some worms so very yummy.

The dessert they get can't be beat,

Seeds of bulgur, durum, barley and wheat,

If mixed with dove's milk, that is just fine,

For then they feel like on cloud nine."

39

Coo, coo, coo , Coo, coo, coo

I hear soft chirping and stomping of feet,

The chicks are hungry and would like to eat,

When fed, their beaks they open nice and wide,

And the booty of the day will be dropped inside.

Quietly alongside the window a seat I find,

Listening to the noise that is coming from behind.

Coo, coo, coo , Coo, coo, coo

Since growing day by day,

Less room in the planter there is for play,

Their buttocks outside the planter

they must place,

So the inside of the nest

doesn't get dirty from waste -

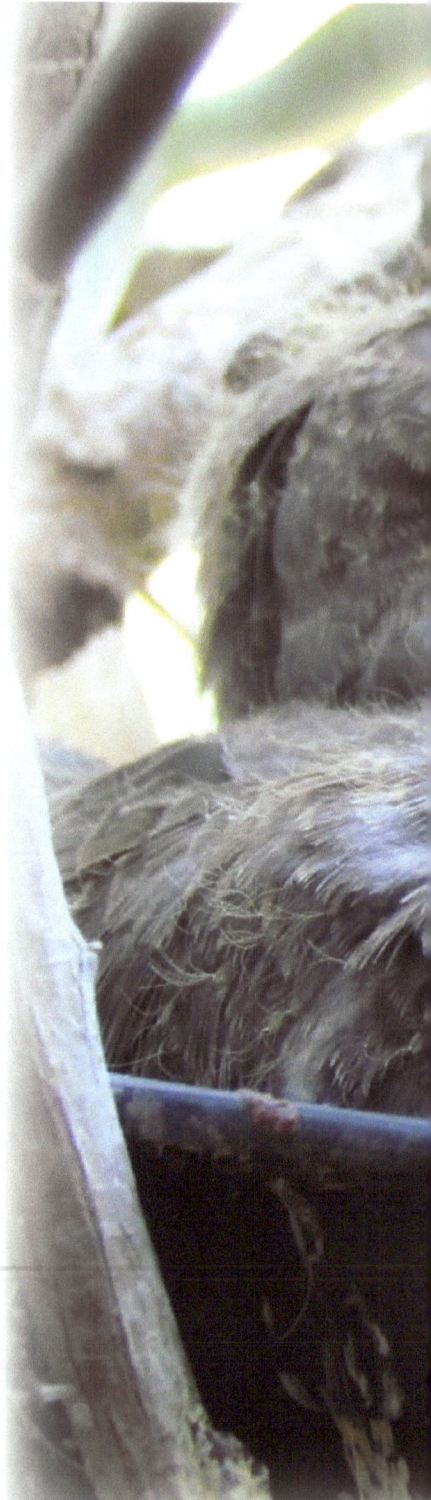

With their parents no longer around,

Who like brooms always cleaned up

without making a sound.

Now they are walking alongside the nest,

Waving their wings while full of zest,

They can't wait to fly high in the sky,

So they flutter their wings as they try.

47

Coo, coo, coo , Coo, coo, coo

Boy, we just had a real close call

Zip to the first floor almost did fall,

Although from danger they were told to stay away,

At times experiments lead them astray,

Doing exercises enthusiastically in order to fly far,

They rattle their wings, tap their feet

and ready they are

Like a pair of fearless acrobats they do act,

Who get an applause from the audience,

and that is a fact.

49

They remind me of their father during courtship,

When their beautiful mother gave him such hardship,

To impress his girlfriend is what he tried,

Bragging and showing off with her at his side,

High in the wind he flew,

Higher and higher into the wild blue,

Then down like a parachute he did glide,

And next to her he landed with pride.

51

It is no wonder that from the window we heard,

His courting sound to his female bird,

Soon they became a lovely pair,

The moon and stars their love did share,

A match made in heaven truly indeed,

As they winked to each other and then agreed,

Their radiance spread all over their face,

And under a shining canopy the wedding took place.

Coo, coo, coo , Coo, coo, coo

Zip and Zippy are maturing to their prime,

And mother leaves them for longer periods of time,

Perhaps for a long walk she goes,

Or to a puddle of water to refresh her toes,

Their sadness is gone
 in case return she may never,
Because return she will
forever and ever.

Quiet and silence from the nest
to the ground,
Away flew mother and the chicks
nowhere around,

"Goodbye doves

we'll meet again one day,

During the next nesting season

which is not far away."

61

More information about the laughing-dove:

63

It is no wonder that in some Arab and African nations,

The laughing-dove has been turned

into a holy creation,

The Muslims keep the doves in a pen,

And like a precious animal they care for them,

Many say that in the chirping of the bird,

Evening prayers and blessings can be heard,

If you listen carefully to the cooing of the dove,

In any language it means,"

Blessed be the one Above."*

*"Ushkuru Rabkum" from an Arabic prayer

Into their mosques and holy places

they were taken,

And our holy land in the last century

they have not forsaken,

Some say they came by a natural drive,

And that from North Africa they did arrive,

Either which way, by us she loves to be,

And she gives lots of joy to our family.

Such dedicated parents as these,

With father helping, always ready to please,

By building the nests his love he proved,

And from the side of his mate he never moved,

Mornings and afternoons the eggs he did incubate,

To prove he is a good father and a wonderful mate.

Let me tell you how the story will end,

The nineteen-day-old chicks for themselves

begin to fend,

They'll spread their wings and begin to fly,

but have no fear,

For the time being mother and father

will watch them from near,

Next to their parents for a while longer

they will rest,

Until their independence they are ready to test.

General information about the laughing-dove

- The laughing-dove is from the pigeon family. There are sixteen different species of doves of which the laughing-dove is one of them and the most common in Israel.

- The laughing-dove lays her eggs approximately three to four times a year, between February and August. They lay two eggs at a time. At first only one egg comes out and only after the second egg comes out, do they begin incubating them (sitting on them).

- Laughing-doves soften grains and seeds in their crop (throats) which after a while they become "dove's milk." It is this milk mixed with other grains and seeds that the baby doves eat until five days old.

- The parents empty their dove's milk directly into their chicks' mouths. Once they mature the doves begin to eat other grains and seeds. They eat the dove's milk until they are twelve days old.

- The dove is different from other birds as they know how to sip and swallow water. If you want to raise doves that you may find, just place a bowl of water and they will come to drink from the water.

Talia Berkovich-Zehavi

Who is sitting at my window?

http://bztalia.wix.com/books

facebook: ‏מי שם בחלון?‏

bztalia@gmail.com

Thank you for reading my book! If you found it informational and enjoyable,
I would really appreciate it if you left me a review at Amazon.com